قلب قوي

# A Strong Heart

A book of stories and dreams for the future by Syrian and Palestinian children living in County Mayo

A Kids' Own Book

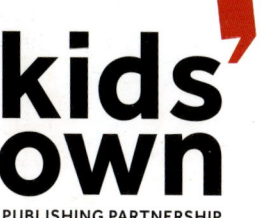

A Strong Heart:
A book of stories and dreams for the future by Syrian and Palestinian children living in County Mayo
©Kids' Own Publishing Partnership CLG, 2018

All rights reserved.
No part of this book may be reproduced or transmitted in any form without prior written authorisation.

ISBN 9781902432984

Published by:
Kids' Own Publishing Partnership CLG
40 Wolfe Tone Street, Sligo, Co. Sligo, F91 R231, Ireland
(+353) 71 9170759
www.kidsown.ie
Charity number: 20639

Kids' Own editorial team:
Jo Holmwood, Emma Kavanagh, Alice Lyons

Design:
Martin Corr

Text & images:
All text and images by participating children

Project writer:
Mary Branley

Project artist:
Vanya Lambrecht Ward

Acknowledgements:
Kids' Own would like to thank all the children for their participation and collaboration on this project: Aya, Ali, Khaled, Ibrahim, Yousef, Alaa, Yahya, Amer, Rashed, Hamza, Amal, Mohamad, Lina, Rahaf, Ritaj, Sidrat. Thanks also to their families for supporting their engagement with us. A special thanks to Rachel Mansour, Michelle O'Mahoney and Patricia Quinn from South West Mayo Development Company, who have supported the development and delivery of this project in County Mayo. Thanks also to Orla O'Neill and Karen Ryan from St Stephen's Green Trust and to Orla Henihan and the staff at Linenhall Arts Centre, Castlebar, for allowing us to use their community space. We are grateful for additional support from Siofra Kilcullen at Mayo County Council and Jody Clarke, Senior External Relations Associate at the UNHCR. Thanks also to Orla Kenny, Jim Power and Context Language Solutions. Thanks to writer Mary Branley and artist Vanya Lambrecht Ward for all their work on the project.

This project has been generously funded by St Stephen's Green Trust and South West Mayo Development Company, with additional support from the Linenhall Arts Centre, Castlebar.

Also generously supported by Mayo County Council.

# Welcome to our book

# مرحبًا بك في كتابنا

We are children who have fun together. We were born in Syria or Palestine before we came to Ireland. We all speak many languages, including Arabic.

We made this book to be famous. We hope you will enjoy learning about our lives.

# Friendship الصداقة

### Aya

I like this group because Alaa is my new friend, but Amal is my old friend for two years. We met at the hotel in Ireland and we played together. Happy memories. It's lovely to see her again and I'm so happy.

I like to see all my friends again from Westport and Castlebar. We get to see each other and make things and tell stories.

### Sidrat

All the third class are my friends.

### Amer

There are no problems in Ireland. I've done a lot of travelling in my life, but I would not say that it was hard. You fly from country to country, and it is fine when you are with your family. You make friends everywhere you go and then you get a bit sad when you have to leave and you have to make new friends. Here I have five friends.

### Khaled

I go to the park every single day with Sean, my friend. He is in the same class as me and he is actually the best at football. We kick the ball around with his brother Cian. I like Cian as well. He is in Ali's class. We play world cup and everyone is against each other. I choose Manchester United, Sean picks Chelsea and Cian picks Arsenal. It doesn't matter who wins because we are all friends together.

### Amer عامر

I am eleven years old and I live in Ballina. It's a good town for everything, especially the river. I like to look at the river and see the ducks and fish jump. One day I saw a really big fish jump out of the water. It was a salmon.

My dream for the future is to be a policeman, because a policeman is good for catching people who break the law. When I grow up, I don't know where I might live, maybe Ireland or Turkey.

I lived in Turkey for three years before I came to Ireland. I like Turkey. The sun is hot and the beaches are lovely. Then we travelled from Turkey to Greece. In Greece the sun is hot too, the beaches were really lovely. The homes were like Ireland.

# Rashed راشد

My name is **Rashed** and I live in Ballina. I am thirteen years old. I like drawing. The most important thing about me is that I'm good at basketball, because I'm tall. I make the baskets.

Ballina is a big town with a long river, good for salmon. I've been there nine months and my family was very happy to come to Ballina, and County Mayo is a nice county. My dream for the future is to be a businessman, selling cars, BMW, Porsches and Audis and all the sports cars. I love to drive fast and I'm learning. First I have to learn the theory and then do my driving test.

Ballina

قلب قوي  A Strong Heart

Ballina

### Lina لينا

I am twelve years old and I live in Ballina. The people are very, very nice and said welcome. I like school and I'm in fourth class. My teacher is very nice. My best thing in school is spelling and handwriting.

### Rahaf رهف

My name is Rahaf and I am fourteen years old. I live in Ballina. I love it because everyone is kind and nice and I love Ireland because it's my other country. Syria is first and Ireland is my other country.

My dream for the future is to be a doctor and I'd love to dance, but I can't. I have problems in my muscles and we are not sure if it will get better. I went to London to do a special blood test but we have not got the result yet.

We still have a lot of family in Syria and when the war is over, we will go and visit them.

# Food

الطعام

### Hamsa
Syrian bread is good. It is different to Irish bread. But I like Irish bread now. I have Nutella on it. I went shopping yesterday with my mother. I bought Oreos and other things. My Mum bought food for the family. She makes lovely food for us. My favourite is a big sandwich with meat and tomatoes and mayonnaise and salad. I'd like to be a chef when I'm older and make spaghetti and Syrian food.

### Ritaj
We eat Syrian food, like special leaves cooked until they turn soft and black. Then you put lemon on it. My favourite food is Syrian, chicken and rice and a special yellow sauce. My Mammy and Daddy like spicy sauce, but not me.

### Aya
My favourite food is garlic and lemon with hot Syrian bread. We call it "burnt fingers". We make it every week.

### Lina
My favourite food is spaghetti and tomato sauce.

### Yousef
I like pepperoni pizza. I also love burger, chips and coke, and chicken sandwiches.

### Ibrahim
My favourite food is an apple.

### Amal
When we celebrate Eid we make delicious food. One of my favourite meals is from Turkey; vine leaves with meat and rice. Then you squeeze lemon juice over it.

### Khaled
My favourite food is chicken kebab. Alaa and Rahaf love margarita pizzas, burgers and chips.

# Khaled خالد

I am twelve years old. I live in Claremorris in the middle of Mayo. It's a big town. I live with my family. Ahmed, my big brother is fourteen. Ali is my little brother, and my sister Rahme is three. She is the boss. When we go outside she always wants to come out with us, and if we don't let her, she throws water at the television. She goes into my room and takes my stuff out of my bag and throws it out the window. Fatima is my biggest sister and she is seventeen. My mum's name is Shamsa.

My dream for the future is to be a footballer first and play for Ireland. When I'm thirty three, I will be a teacher and go back to Syria to teach English.

I got two new pets this week, two rabbits, a male and a female. If they have babies we will keep them. They like carrots. They are really funny and mess. Ali fell on them in the shed. They go under the shed and play hide and seek with us. They love to run in our big garden. I have the biggest garden in the whole of Claremorris.

I like marbles. We played them in Syria too. If you hit them you win the other person's marble. Then you have loads.

A Strong Heart قلب قوي

## Ali

I am ten years old. I live with Khaled in Claremorris.

I want to be a pilot in a helicopter and rescue people when they have broken legs, and bring them to hospital. You have to learn how to drive it.

I play football. I am good at scoring goals. We need a referee sometimes when we fight over the ball, or if it was a hand ball.

## Mohamad محمد

I am ten years old. I live in Claremorris. It's a good place to live because there are lots of children to play football with. My birthday is on Wednesday, April 18th. My Mum will make me a cake.

### عيد ميلاد سعيد
### Happy Birthday in Arabic

We have a lovely lake in Claremorris and we walk and cycle around it. Some people fish there and they get a lot of pike. Beside the lake there is playground and a new hospital. It's lovely and big. There are a lot of things to play on; two pitches, one big and one small, a pitch to play football, and tennis.

When I grow up my dream is to be a doctor in town and help people. I have two sisters, one born on Christmas Eve in 2017, Basma بسمة and she is only three months. She is a very good baby and doesn't cry a lot. She is very cute. She likes to play a lot with her hands, and she is always smiling. Her name Basma means smiling.

# Ramadan

رمضان

### Amal, Alaa and Mohamad

Ramadan is twenty-nine or thirty days, it depends on the moon. We fast all the days and eat at night. The reason we do this is that we feel what poor people feel, who are without money and can't buy food in so many countries. At four o'clock, we have a bit of food in the morning. We don't drink any water during the day or anything. When we finish fasting, we celebrate Small Eid, العيد الصغير when the moon is full. Eid is three days and after that there are two months and a half and then we celebrate Big Eid, العيد الكبير That is for four days.

We fast because we are Muslim and during the night, we pray twelve times. We put our prayer mats on the ground and kneel, we stand and we sit.

We don't find it difficult. We feel happy doing it. We feel happy saying our prayers so we don't feel hungry. Doctors say it's a very good thing to fast so your body is free of sickness and lots of things. When you fast you make your body thin.

Our prayers are from the Koran, our religion book.

Young children under age seven are not allowed to fast. We eat a lot of sweets at Eid and our parents and friends give us a lot of money. We give people meat, we kill a lamb or a sheep and cook very delicious food.

We don't get thirsty because every day it rains in Ireland. If you sleep two hours, you don't feel hungry. You can eat at four o'clock in the morning and not after that.

A Strong Heart قلب قوي

# Westport

## Alaa علاء

My name is Alaa and I am living in Westport for two years. It's a very nice place and I like the beach. We go to Westport House and go on the water slide into the pond. I always scream and laugh when I go down the slide. School makes me laugh too. Yesterday we were painting a plate and turned it over to make a print of a flower in red and pink.

My dream for the future is to be a teacher of maths and I want to be a nice teacher to everyone. I wouldn't be cross to the children at all. But if the children are naughty, I will have to be a little bit cross. I would like to have my own family too. I would like my family to be happy and be nice to them.

My greatgrandmother is 111 years old. But she can run and walk and if you look at her she looks twenty-five years younger. She eats lots of healthy food. She lives in Syria. We speak to her on the phone. My grandmother looks like 100 but she is sixty-five and she can't walk. Her mother can run more than her.

A Strong Heart قلب قوي

# Westport

### Yahya يحيى

My name is Yahya. I am thirteen years old. I live in Westport. Life is good because I have a brother and friends. I play games.

My dream for the future is to be a footballer and a boxer. I would like to be a policeman in Westport. I would be a nice policeman helping people not to do wrong.

Syria has different flags that mean different things.

A Strong Heart قلب قوي

# Westport

## Ritaj رتاج

My name is Ritaj and I am nine years old. Sidrat is my sister. I like Westport because it is near the beach and sometimes we walk there, and in the summer we go swimming. Sometimes the water is freezing.

I am in second class, and my teacher tells me I'm very good at my work; at English and Maths. I love Art and helping the teacher.

When I go home from school, I like to take a nap and lie on the couch. Sidrat wakes me up for dinner.

I'm going to make the world into a swimming pool, and I'm going to make a machine to take all the water from the beach and put it inside the world. I'm going to take Aya with me and Sidrat to live on a different country with nice aliens and monsters and sunshine. When we go on holidays, I'm going to go to the world and swim inside it. We need to have floatees. It's going to be nice weather and sunshine. But that might be a bad idea because sometimes people need to breathe.

## Sidrat سدرة

My name is Sidrat. I live in Westport for two years. I am eleven years old. I like Westport because there are nice people in it. I live with Mounir, my brother, Mayar, my brother, Ritaj, my sister and my Mum and my Dad. School is good and I am getting on well. All the third class are my friends. Art is my favourite subject.

My dream for the future is to be an artist and draw people. Our school is Scoil Phádraig and I hope my teacher picks me to help with the green school. We help children who have not got food or clothes and we clean up the litter. I like to help the teachers in the school and be the best girl in school.

I lived for a year in France; I forget the town. France is nice but you have to learn how to speak French. I forget that now. Then I lived two years in Greece and that's why we came to Ireland.

# War and flight

# الحرب والفرار

## Rahaf

The war started on 15th March 2011. The first battle was in Daraa and the next in Latakia. Assad, the leader of Syria, was fighting against another leader in Syria. They were fighting to see who would be in power.

My family left in 2015, because the Government took my brother five times and when he came home he was not very well. We have just one brother and I don't know why the government did this. After that, my Dad took Mohamad to Turkey and after two months, me, my sister and my mother went to Turkey too, to a place called Mersin.

After eight months, we went to Greece with my family and brother, but the men who were going to bring us to Greece took the money and left us in the jungle. That was frightening.

After that, five people were allowed to go to Greece and my brother said to my Dad, you can go with the girls and Mum and I will stay. And that is what we did. But we have not seen our brother for two years.

After ten months in Greece, we came to Ireland but before that we were in a bad refugee camp. It had snakes. We moved to another camp. After fifteen days, we went to a hotel because by this time I was not well. I was sick because I did not have enough oxygen, because of the wood fires at the camps.

We still have a lot of our family in Syria and when the war is over, we will go for a visit.

# Castlebar

## Amal أمل

My name is Amal; it means Hope. My grandmother is called Amal and my mother is also called Amal. This is an important name in my family. I have three brothers all older than me. The older one is called Fiaras, then Omar and the other one is Mohamad. I live in Castlebar and my teachers tell me I'm keeping up very well with English. I like to learn Irish as it is important to learn it in this country and it is important that it is kept up.

I love reading books and doing questions about the books. It is different in every way from my old school. In Lebanon, we had a different teacher for every subject, but here we have the same teacher in primary school. I'm in fifth class now.

When I was very small, I wanted to be an artist but now that I'm older, I want to be a doctor or a nurse. I would like to help poor people who get hurt to get better. When you are a doctor, you need a strong heart.

Castlebar is not noisy and it's a nice place, but the weather is horrible and even though the summer is coming, the weather is still raining with a little bit of sunshine.

### Hamza حمزة

I am eleven years old and I live in Castlebar with my family; my sister, my brother and my mum. I like this town. School is hard because I am learning English and Irish. I like to play football every day in school, and every time it's sunny, I go to play football with my brother. I like YouTube and games on my brother's laptop.

My dream for the future is to be a football player and be a chef. I'd make any food like spaghetti and Syrian food.

Castlebar

### Yousef يوسف

I am eleven years of age. I live in Castlebar with my family; my mother, two brothers and my sister. My English is getting better all the time.

My dream for the future is to be a doctor; a surgeon. I would like to work in Ireland, Syria, Lebanon and America and Libya. My Mum likes Libya so I would like to visit there.

I like reading because it helps me to know how I can speak in English.

A Strong Heart قلب قوي

Castlebar

### Ibrahim إبراهيم

I am eight years old and I live in Castlebar with my family. I love football, and I like to save goals for my team. I like school and I like art.

When I grow up, I want to be a footballer and get a bulldog.

# Castlebar

## Aya آية

My name is Aya. I live in Castlebar with my family for one year. I like Castlebar because I like school. Castlebar is cold.

My dream for the future is to be an astronaut and fly away when I grow up. I'm going to get all the people to build my rocket. I'm going to take the people I love with me so they will be okay. We will go to another planet and take some oxygen. If something was going to destroy the planet, I'm going to save the earth because I want to do something that no-one has done before. Or maybe I will destroy the planet if no one can save it.

I have two names: Rafa and Aya, but I like Aya more.

My dream for the future is to be a doctor, if I can. I will learn about the body in University. I was in hospital last month. I had to sleep there for one month. I had a very bad virus. I got a bandage and they took blood and gave me medicine. They were so nice to me, the nurses, and the doctors. Five or six girls came with the doctor to help. One of them was the sister to Ali and Khaled. I got sick after for a week when I came home. There was no place for my Mum to pray in the hospital.

## Be kind to everyone
## كن لطيفًا مع الجميع

# How We Made This Book

**16 children invented this book. We met every Saturday for five weeks and three hours. We painted and coloured and made shapes and patterns.**

How you make a pattern: You use lots of shapes to make a picture. Then you take a photo of it. Then you put it on the computer and ask the computer to repeat the picture over and over.

We enjoyed making this book, meeting new friends. We told our stories to **Mary** and she helped us. Vanya helped us with the art. We had lots of fun making this book.

Thank you… Ireland for the money to make this book; **Vanya** and **Mary** for helping us; Rachel and the Linenhall for the workshops.

**By children participating on this project**

With much joy and anticipation, we started the visual work for the book alongside the writing. We always need to warm up our hands and wake up our heads before we can make, especially after a road trip, so what better way than through playfulness; tangrams and other shapes and combinations have endless potential and this transpired into lots and lots of patterns which now form the backgrounds and framing of the other work. Portraits, football, food and other illustrations of the things the children liked best became the subjects of our drawing and painting and hopefully accompany their stories in a way that you can see their enjoyment and infectious joyfulness.

**Vanya Lambrecht Ward**
**Visual artist**

A Strong Heart  قلب قوي

| | |
|---|---|
| Alaa | علاء |
| Ali | علي |
| Amal | أمل |
| Amer | عامر |
| Aya | آية |
| Hamza | حمزة |
| Ibrahim | إبراهيم |
| Khaled | خالد |
| Lina | لينا |
| Mohamad | محمد |
| Rahaf | رهف |
| Rashed | راشد |
| Ritaj | رتاج |
| Sidrat | سدرة |
| Yahya | يحيى |
| Yousef | يوسف |